Lowza
AND THE WORD SHE DIDN'T KNOW

written by
Esmihan Almontaser

illustrated by
Youssef Rahmaoui

Copyright © 2025 by Esmihan Almontaser
Illustrations by Youssef Rahmaoui
All rights reserved.
No part of this publication may be reproduced, distributed, or transmitted in any form or by any means, including photocopying, recording, or other electronic or mechanical methods, without the prior written permission of the publisher, except in the case of brief quotations embodied in critical reviews and certain other noncommercial uses permitted by copyright law.
ISBN: 979-8-9999923-2-1
First Edition
Printed in United States of America
This book is a work of fiction. Any resemblance to actual persons, places, or creatures, living or dead, is purely coincidental.
To reach the author, email ReadYemeniABC@gmail.com

For all the little ones who feel different, may you discover, just like Lowza, that faith can turn sadness and fear into strength.

At nine years old, Lowza loved two things more than anything in the world: her little sister Susu and reading the Qur'an. Every morning, before the city woke up, she would sit cross-legged on her prayer mat with her Qur'an on her lap as she read each word with care.

"Bismillah," she would whisper, and recite the surahs.

This week, like the weeks before, she had been preparing for the big Qur'an competition. Her tajweed was sharp, her memory strong and her heart was full of duas.

Susu (short for Sumayyah), only six years old, had also memorized some surahs.
She was supposed to come to the competition, too.
But today, she was curled up at home with a cold, sipping warm soup.
"Sissy," Sumayyah called as Lowza was preparing to leave.
"Win for both of us, okay?"
Lowza smiled, "Insha'Allah, I'll do my best."

At the door, Mama placed a gentle hand on Lowza's shoulder. She recited a prayer as was the practice, before leaving the house. "Bismillaahi, tawakkaltu 'alallaahi, wa laa hawla wa laa quwwata ' illaa billaah."

In the name of Allah, I place my trust in Allah, and there is no might nor power except with Allah.
Lowza closed her eyes and repeated after her.
Her heart felt calm. She was ready.

Lowza and Mama arrived at the university hall just in time. The building was tall and wide, with long glass windows that shimmered in the light.
A big banner above the door read:
"Annual Citywide Qur'an Competition - Bismillah!"
Inside, the air buzzed with chatter and excitement.

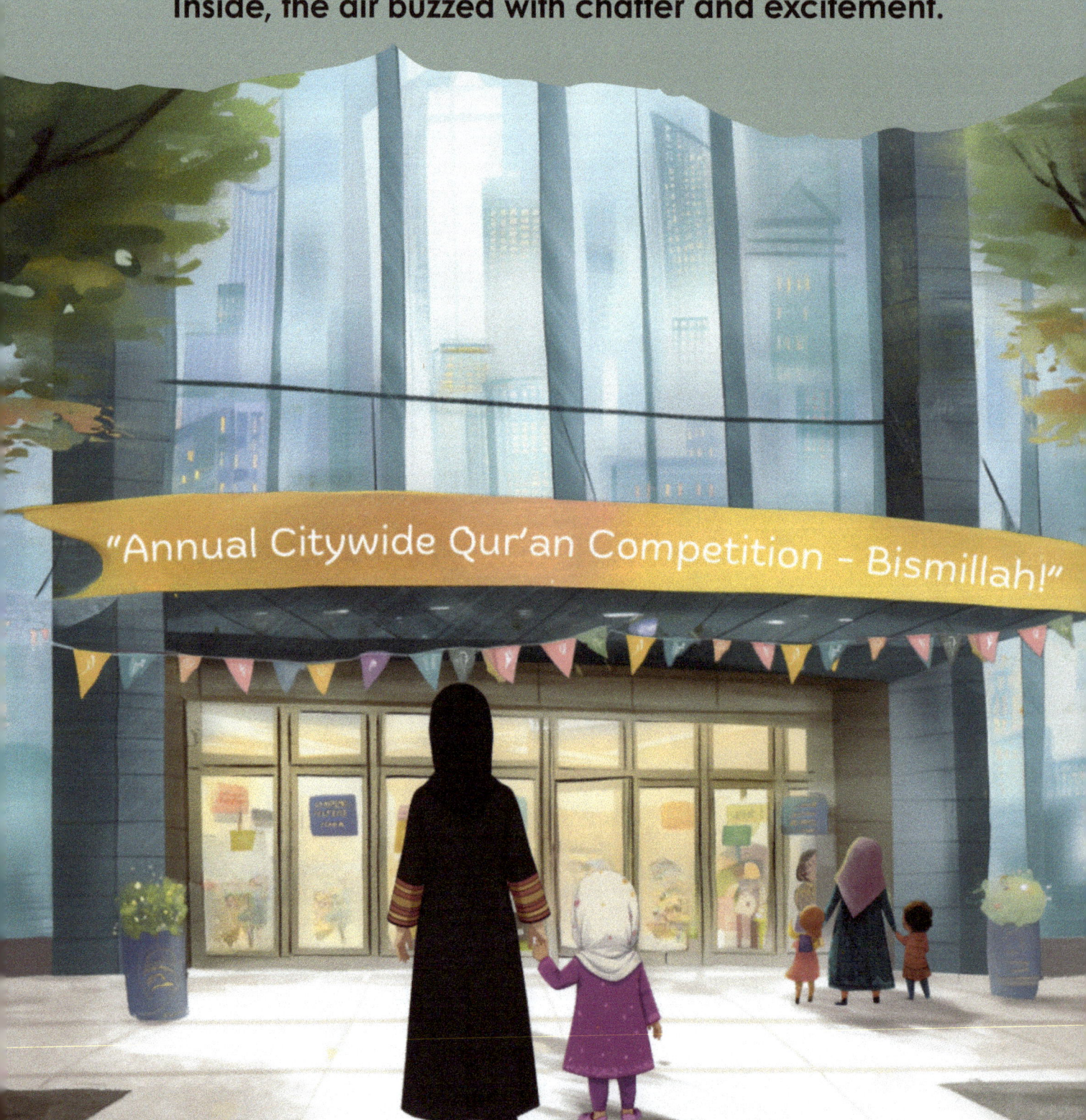

Children filled the hall; some laughing in groups, some practicing quietly with their teachers, and others adjusting their neatly ironed hijabs.
There were also parents holding cameras, and judges with kind eyes. Lowza held loosely to Mama's hand.

"Do you want to go over anything before it starts?" Mama asked gently.

Lowza shook her head. "I think I'm okay. There are so many kids." Many of them seemed to know each other already. They huddled in little groups, whispering and giggling, passing notes and smiles. Most of them wore uniforms from Islamic schools. Lowza could tell right away.

"I've just been studying at home," she murmured. "I don't have classmates here like them."

Mama knelt beside her, brushing a loose curl behind her ear. "And you've worked so hard, habibti. Every surah you've learned, every every letter you've recited, Allah sees it all."
Lowza nodded, but her heart still fluttered nervously.
She remembered a dua she had learned from her teacher.
"Rabbi zidni ilma"
Allah, increase me in knowledge.
She prayed, letting the words settle in her heart.

Just then, the soft crackle of a microphone filled the room and a cheerful voice echoed through the speakers.
"Assalamu alaikum, everyone!"
The hum of chatter stopped. All eyes turned to the front of the hall where a woman in a navy blue abaya smiled brightly from the stage.
"Is everyone excited to be here?" she asked, her voice full of warmth.
Some children nodded shyly. Others clapped politely.

"This is a special day," the woman continued. "Each of you has worked so hard to get here. You've memorized the words of Allah, and that is something to be proud of."

Lowza felt Mama's hand on her shoulder, gentle and steady. "We will select the top three finalists today," the woman said, "but always remember, just by being here, you are already a winner."

A soft breeze seemed to pass through Lowza's chest.
She felt her breath deepen.
Then came the call: "First group, please come forward."
Lowza wasn't in the first group. She wasn't in the second one either.

She watched from her seat as the first few girls walked up to the stage one by one, their voices rising and falling in careful rhythm. Some stumbled. Others glowed with confidence.
A few had to start over.

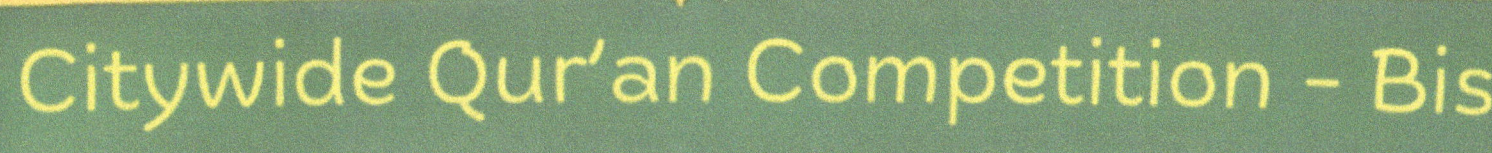

Lowza's turn came in the third group.
She began her recitation, her voice trembling at first,
but steadying with each verse.

When she finished, she bowed her head respectfully, and returned to her seat beside Mama.
"You did beautifully," Mama whispered.

After a pause, she asked, "Would you like to take a break?"
Lowza nodded.
They went out to the university courtyard which had been transformed into a lovely bazaar.

There were tables along the walkways covered in colorful cloths.
There were long, flowing abayas the color of the night sky. Others were purple and blue with shiny threads along the sleeves.

One table had rows of tiny glass bottles filled with pretty-smelling perfumes.
Each one sparkled under the sun. Lowza leaned closer to one and took a deep breath, "This one smells like Eid."
Mama laughed. "That's your Khaloo Adil's favorite."

The next table had on it samosas and bowls of biryani. A lady offered a sample of warm baklava dripping with honey.
"Can we try one?" she asked with wide eyes.
Mama smiled and gave her a napkin, "Just one, for now."

They wandered past families chatting in different languages and children discussing their medals from past years.
They heard vendors calling out.
Then, something caught Lowza's eye. A sign posted in bold letters.

"If you or someone you know experiences Islamophobia, please contact the administration immediately."
Next to the sign, was a table with pamphlets and a gentleman standing nearby.
Lowza tagged her mother's sleeve, "Mama… What's the word? Islam… phobia?"

Mama looked at the sign and grew quiet for a moment.
"It means fear," she said gently. "Islamophobia is when people are afraid of Muslims or Islam.
Sometimes, when people are afraid of something they don't understand, they say or do hurtful things."
Lowza blinked. "But... Why would anyone be afraid of us?
We are just... normal."

If you or someone you know experiences Islamophobia, please contact the administration immediately.

Mama nodded. "Yes, my love. Islam teaches us peace, kindness, and truth. But not everyone knows that. Some people hear things that aren't true, or they don't take the time to learn.
And sometimes, fear makes people act in ways they shouldn't."
Lowza was quiet.
The perfume and baklava didn't seem as exciting anymore.
A strange feeling settled in her stomach, like a pebble that wouldn't go away.

"Do they think we're bad?" she asked softly.
Mama wrapped an arm around her.
"Some might. But many more don't.
That's why being proud of who you are, and sharing the truth with kindness, is so important. You're helping already, just by being you."

As the sun began to dip lower in the sky, someone called out,
"Participants, please return to the hall.
The last round is about to begin."
Lowza held Mama's hand a little tighter as they walked back
through the buzzing bazaar.
She couldn't stop thinking about the sign.
Why would anyone be afraid of Muslims? Do people think I'm scary?
Just because I love the Qur'an and wear a hijab?

Inside the hall, she sat next to Mama, her heart feeling cloudy.
"Mama," she whispered, "what if some people don't like me…
just because I'm Muslim?"
Mama looked at her kindly. "Even the Prophet Muhammad, peace be upon him, was treated unfairly by some people. But he never stopped being kind, patient, and proud of who he was."
Lowza thought about that.
She looked around the room at all the children.

So many faces, so many families, all brought together by the same Book. Then something clicked in her mind as she thought about her Mama's words.

"Phobia" means fear. Maybe it didn't always mean hate. Fear doesn't have to turn into hate, but if no one helps them understand what they fear, it might.

She sat up straighter. That's why I have to be brave. So people can see what Islam really is.

Her thoughts were interrupted when one of the judges started announcing the winners.

"In third place..." he began. Lowza held her breath. A name was called. A girl in a green dress jumped up and ran to the stage. Polite applause filled the room.

"In second place..." Another name. Another round of clapping. Lowza pressed her hands together in her lap.

"And now," the judge said, "in first place, for exceptional clarity, beautiful tajweed, and heartfelt recitation..."

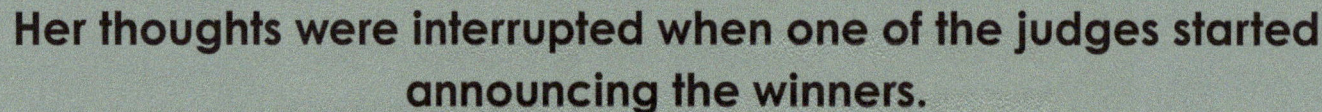

A pause. Then— "Lowza Ahmed!"
She blinked. For a moment, the room went still in her ears.
Then, she felt Mama's arms wrap around her.
"Alhamdulillah," Mama whispered.
Lowza stood and walked to the front. Her heart beat fast, but her steps were steady. The medal was placed around her neck, and the judge handed her a certificate and a warm smile.
"You recited from the heart," he said kindly. "Never stop doing that."

After the ceremony, Mama helped her choose a small box of samosas from the bazaar.

They also visited a nearby table where extra participation medals were being handed out to children who had missed their turn. "For my sister," Lowza explained. "She was too sick to come."

At home, Sumayyah was waiting on the couch, a blanket around her shoulders and a tissue in hand. Lowza tiptoed in with her treasures.
"I have something for you" she said.
Susu sat up. "Did you win?"
Lowza nodded, then knelt beside her and placed the box in her lap.
"And this," she said, holding up the second medal, "is yours."
Susu's eyes widened. "For me?"

"You practiced too. You worked so hard. You were part of this."
Susu stood in front of the mirror, the medal around her neck, smiling so wide it crinkled her nose.
"I look like a winner!" she said, sniffling happily. "You are one," Lowza said softly.

That night, after Susu had fallen asleep, Lowza lay in bed staring up at the ceiling. She thought about the sign she had seen, and the word she hadn't known before. Islamophobia. It still made her feel a little heavy inside. But now, it didn't just feel scary. It felt like something she could help change, not with shouting or anger, but with her kindness, her voice, and her love for the Qur'an. "Maybe they're just waiting to meet someone like me," she whispered. And with that, she closed her eyes, and went to sleep.

What is Islam?

Did you know that Islam is one of the major religions in the world? The people who follow Islam are called Muslims and they believe in one God - Allah. In Islam, Prophet Mohammad (peace be upon him) was the last messenger sent by God to teach people how to live good and kind lives. Islam is about honesty, respect and caring for others no matter where they are from and what they believe.

Islam is followed by over two billion people around the world. They speak many languages, wear different clothes, and live in many ways — but all try to follow the same message of peace, faith, and doing good. Muslims also have five important duties, called the Five Pillars, that guide how they live their lives.

1. Shahada (belief)
Muslims believe in one God and that Muhammad is His final prophet.
2. Salah (prayer)
Muslims pray five times a day to connect with God.
3. Zakat (charity)
Muslims give a part of their money to help those in need.
4. Sawm (fasting in Ramadan)
During the month of Ramadan, Muslims fast from sunrise to sunset to learn self-control and remember the poor.
5. Hajj (pilgrimage)
If they are able, Muslims travel once in their life to the city of Mecca in Saudi Arabia to pray with others from around the world.

The word Islam comes from 'Salaam' which means peace. Islam teaches peace, kindness and respect. Muslims are to treat all people with fairness and never to hurt others. Muslims are taught to treat others with love and care, and never to hurt anyone. If someone tries to harm them, they are allowed to protect themselves but only in a way that is fair and gentle, never out of anger or revenge.

Glossary

Abaya:
A long, loose dress often worn by Muslim women, especially in parts of the Middle East. It can be plain or beautifully decorated.

Allah:
Allah is the Arabic word for God.

Baklava:
A sweet dessert made of thin layers of pastry filled with chopped nuts and soaked in honey or syrup. It's often served on special occasions.

Biryani:
A flavorful rice dish made with spices and sometimes meat or vegetables. It's popular in many South Asian homes.

Bismillah:
This means "In the name of Allah." Muslims use this phrase before reading Qur'an, eating, playing, or starting a new task, big or small.

Dua:
A prayer. Muslims make duas to ask Allah for help, guidance or blessings.

Habibti:
An Arabic word that means "my dear" or "my darling." It's often used to show love and affection.

Hijab:
A headscarf worn by many Muslim girls and women to cover their hair as part of their faith.

Khaloo:
This means "uncle" in Arabic; your mother's brother.

Salaam:
A word that means "peace" in Arabic. It's also part of the Muslim greeting, Assalamu alaikum, which means "peace be upon you."

Samosa:
A crispy, triangle-shaped snack filled with spiced potatoes, meat or vegetables. It is often eaten during Ramadan or at special events.

Surah:
A chapter in the Qur'an, the holy book of Islam. The Qur'an has 114 surahs in total.

Tajweed:
The special way Muslims learn to pronounce and recite the Qur'an with care and beauty, following rules for every sound.

www.ingramcontent.com/pod-product-compliance
Lightning Source LLC
Chambersburg PA
CBHW041218130526
44582CB00026BA/91